The Colours of Madhubani (Colouring Book)

Shinjini Thakur

ISBN: 1984956493
ISBN-13: 978-1984956491

DEDICATION

The Book is dedicated to my dear daughter Tia.

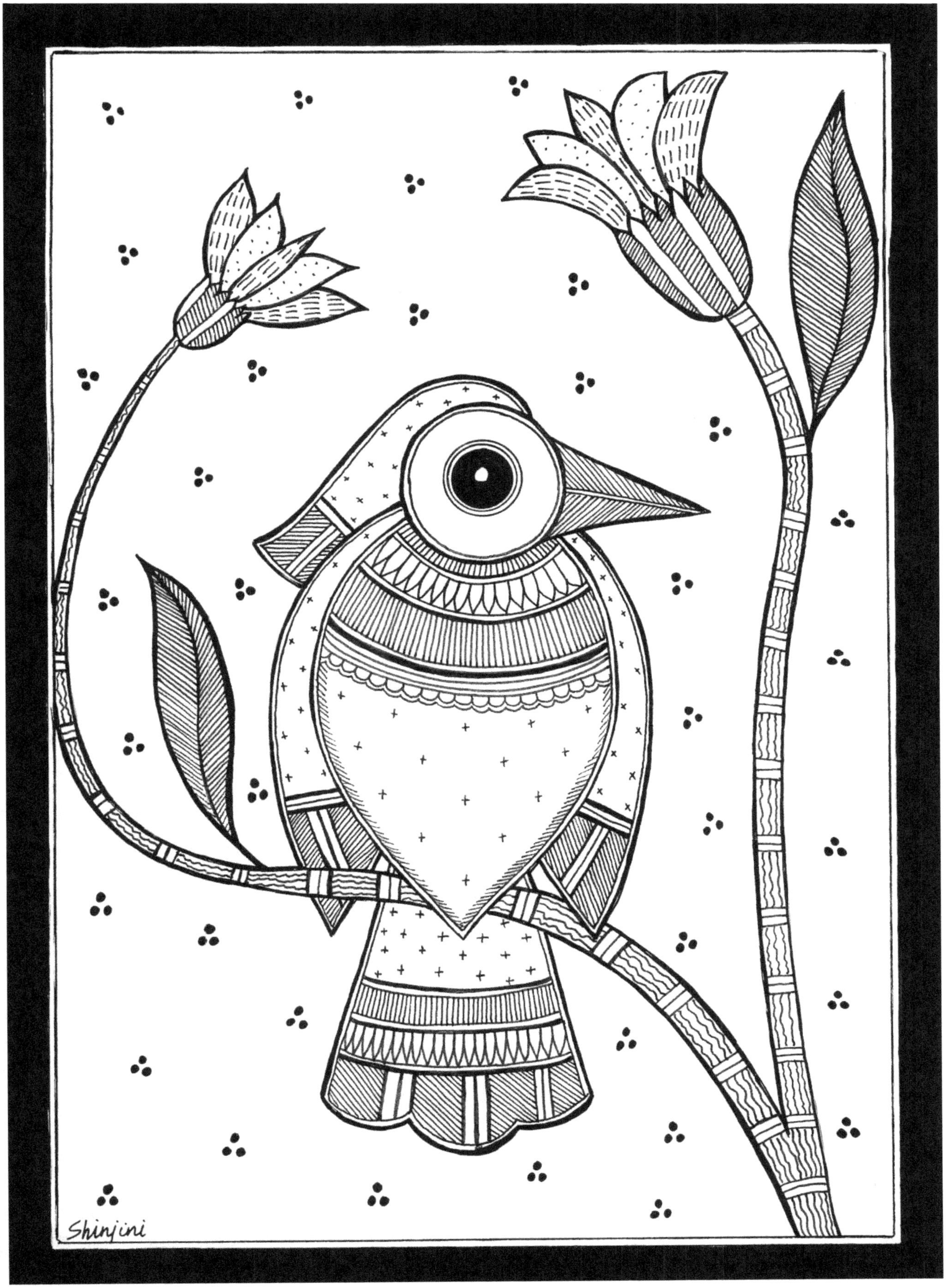
Shinjini

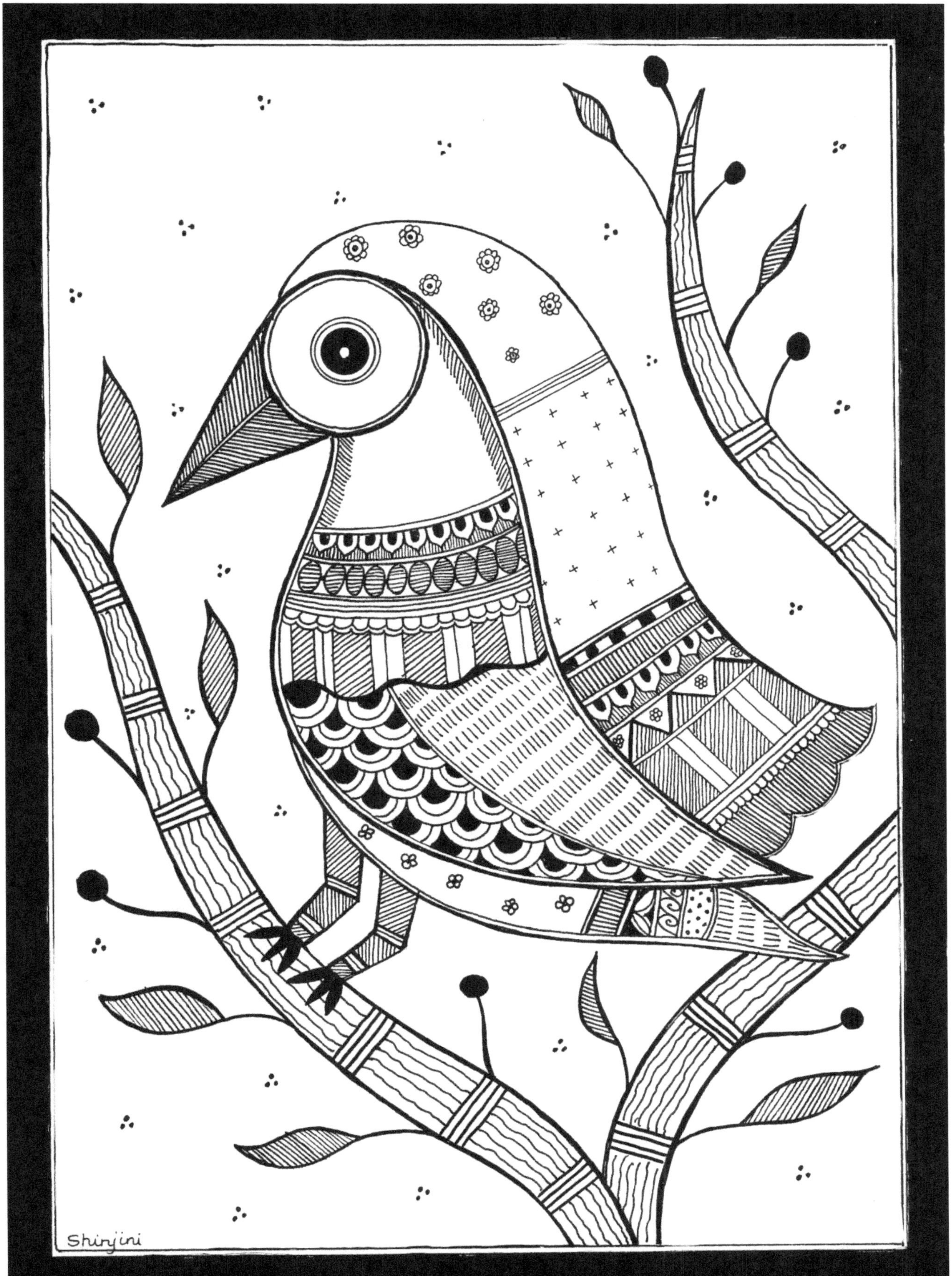
Shinjini

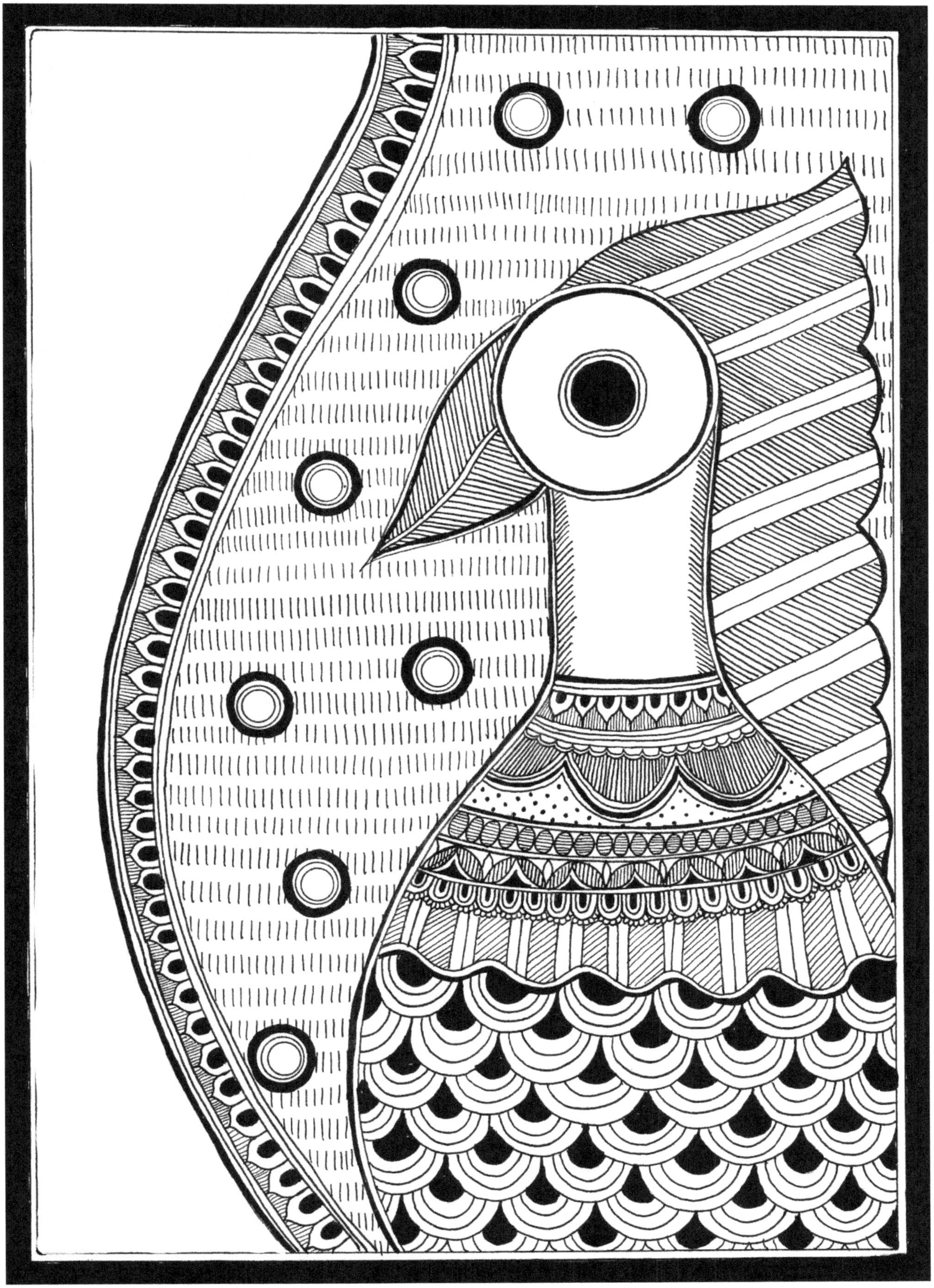

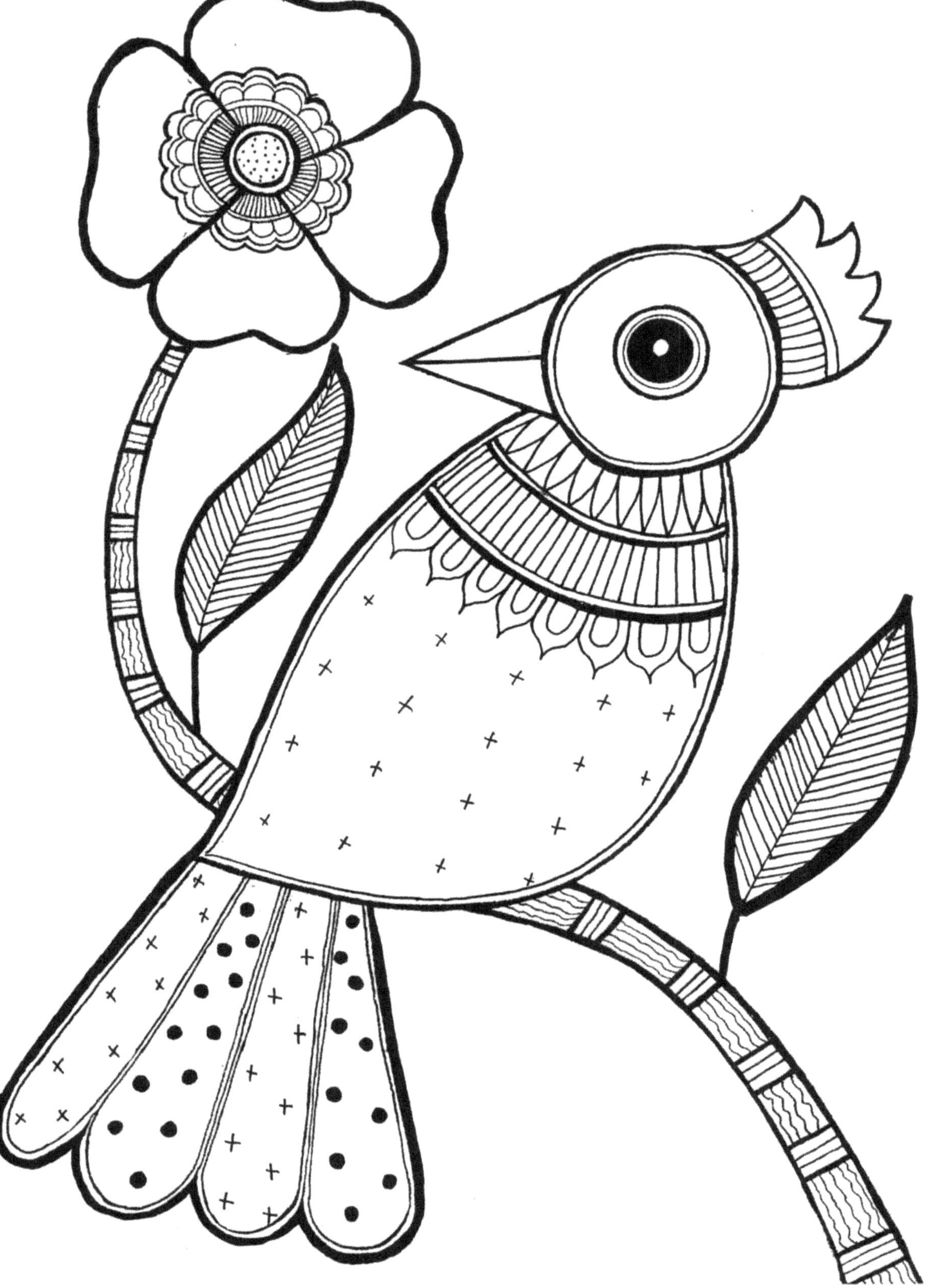

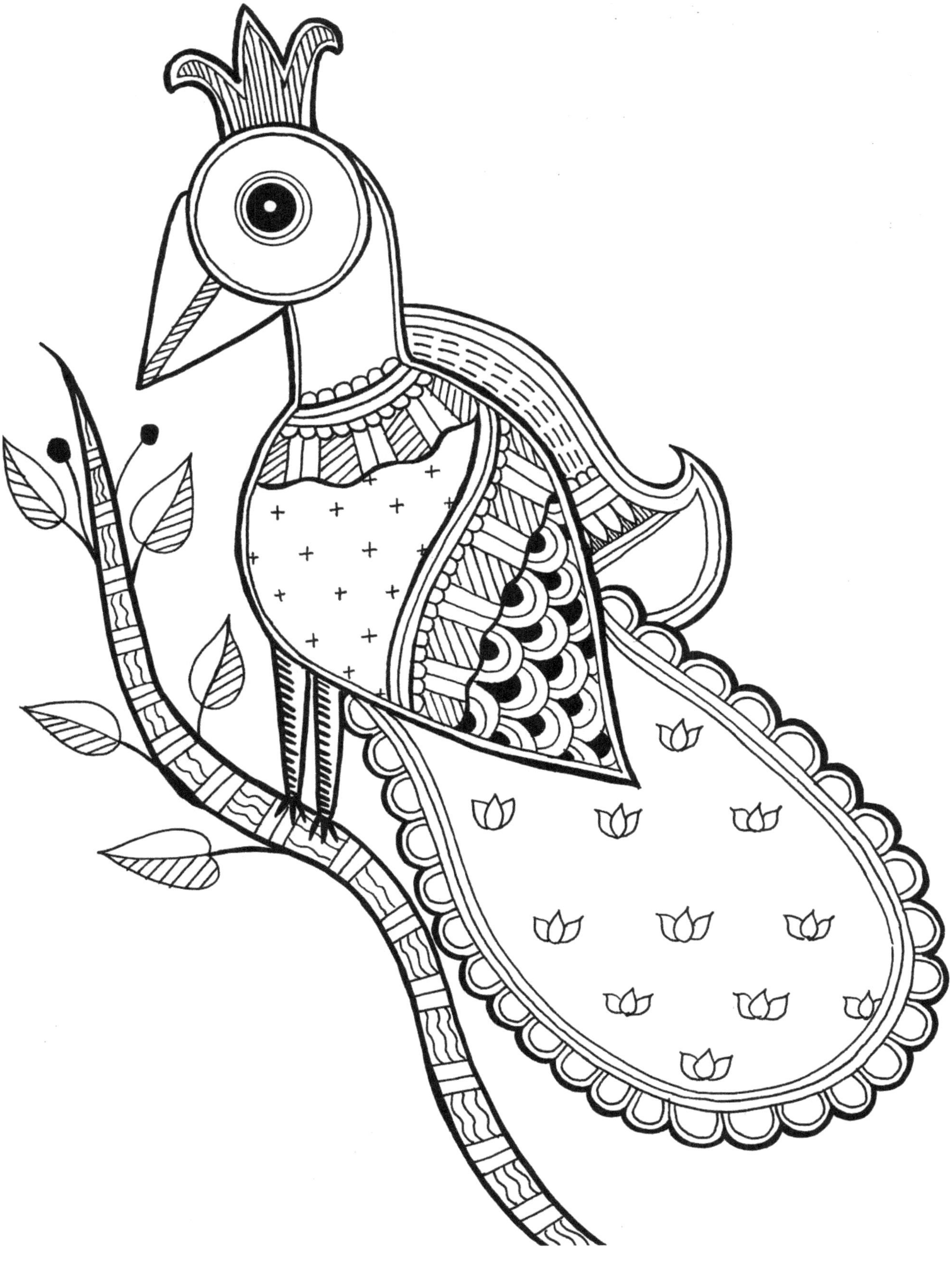

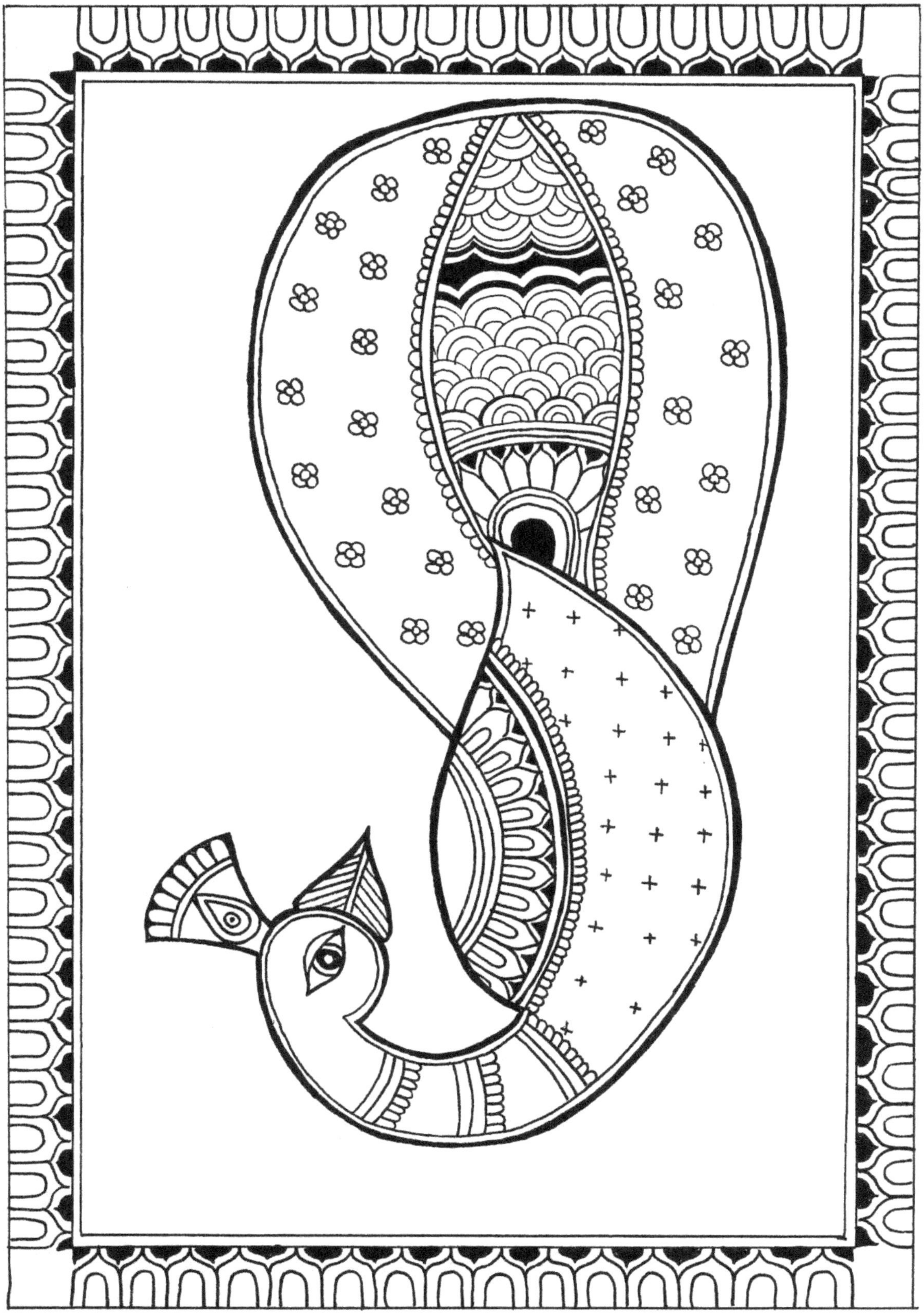

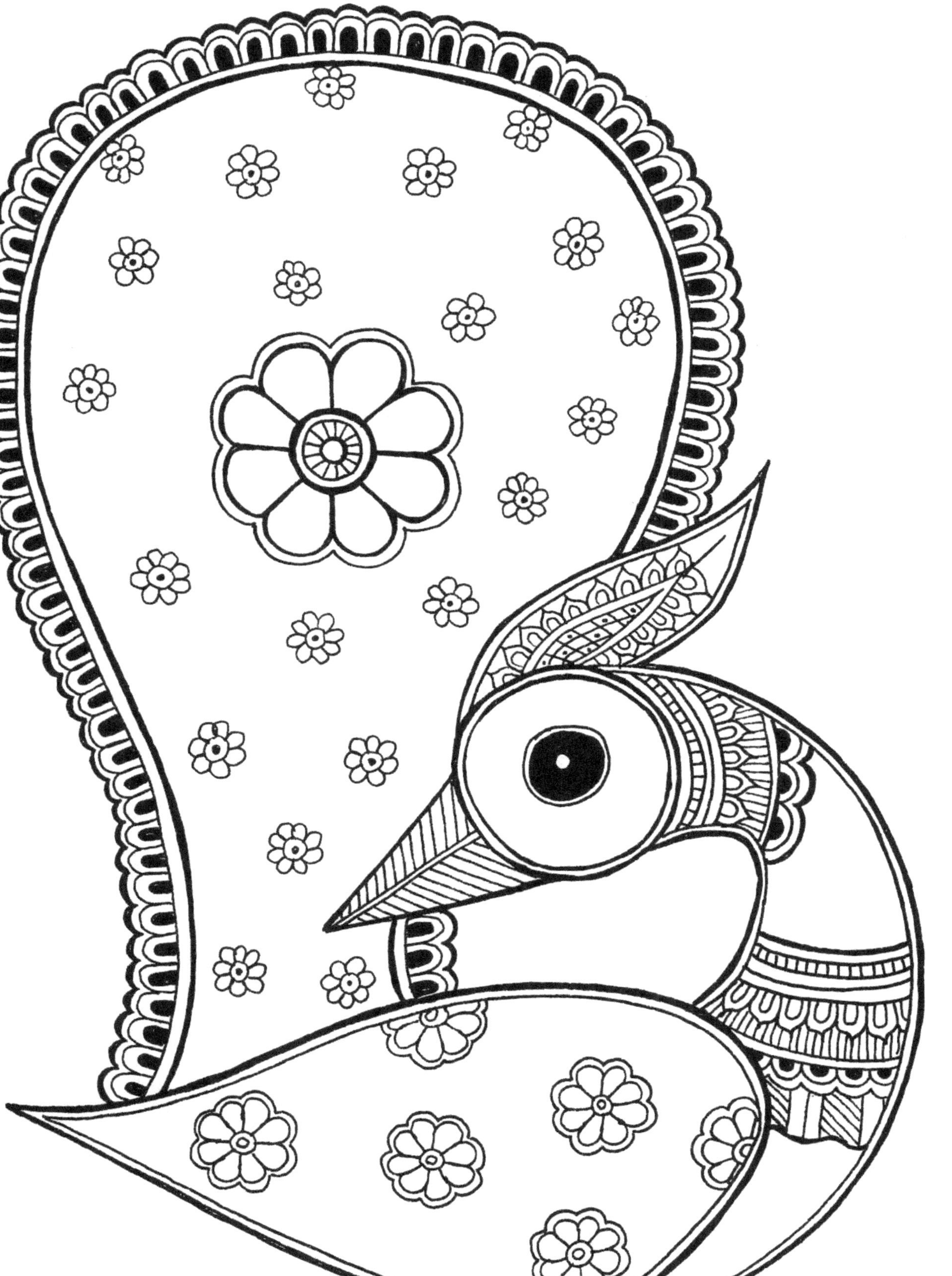

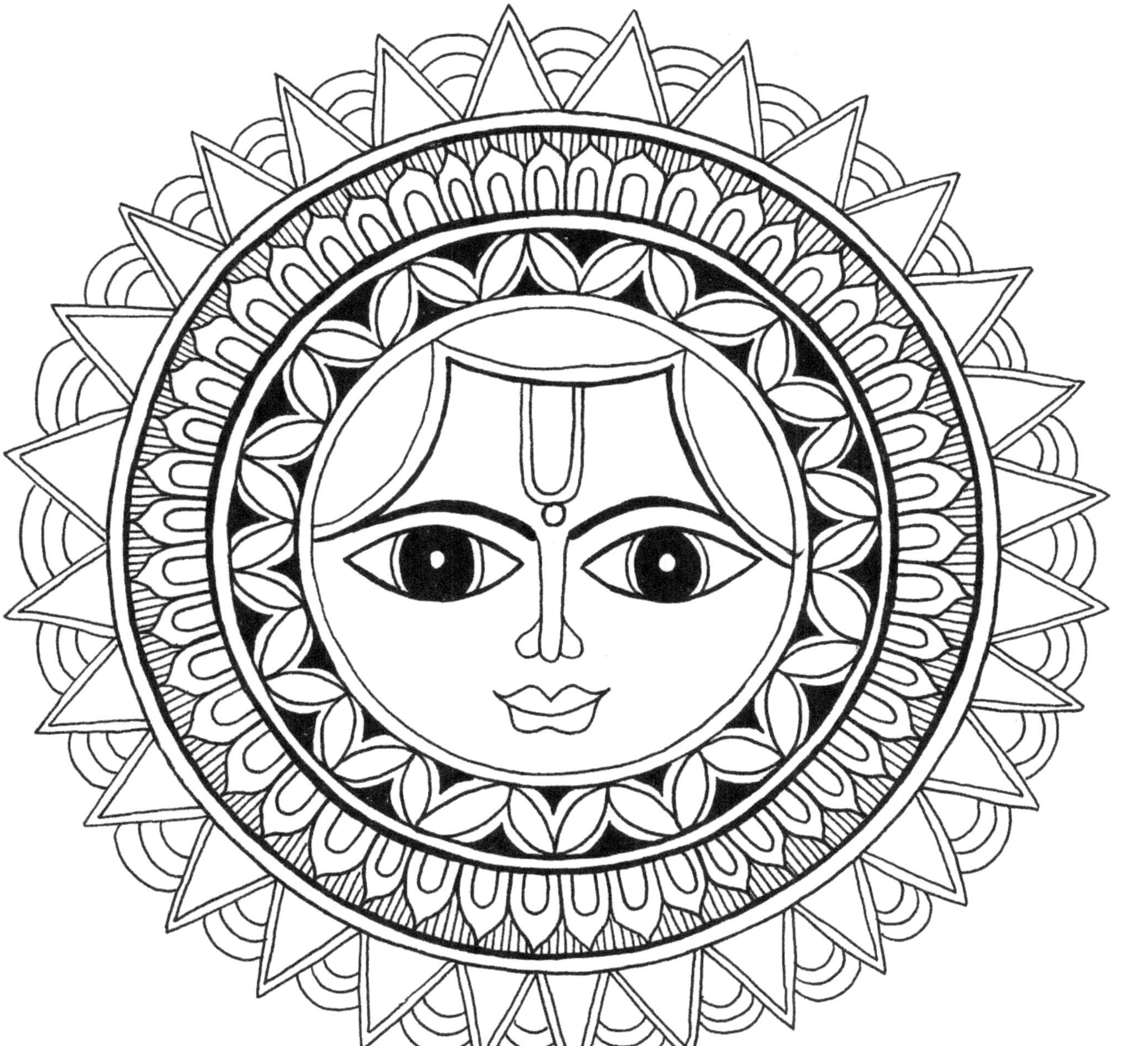

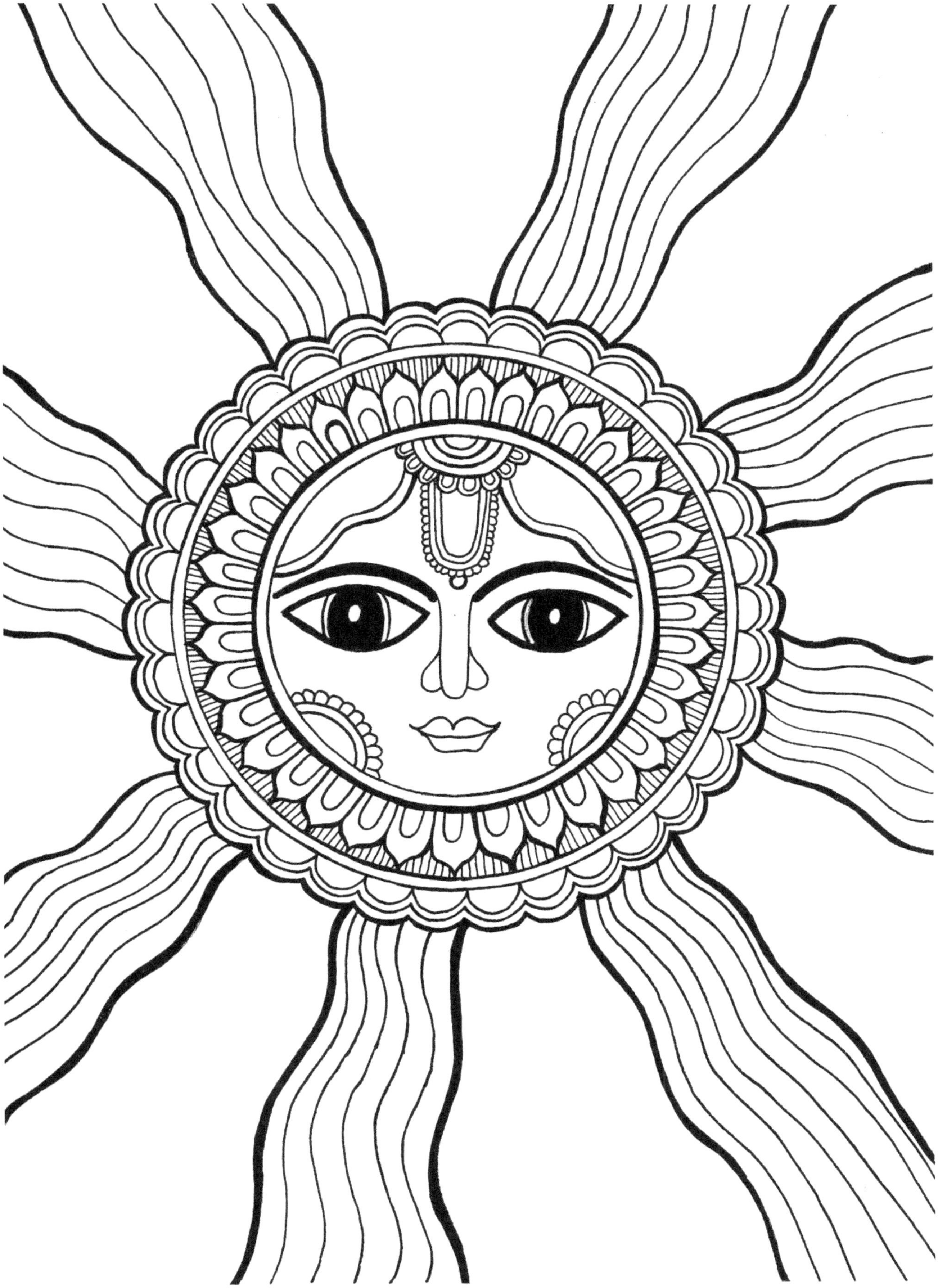

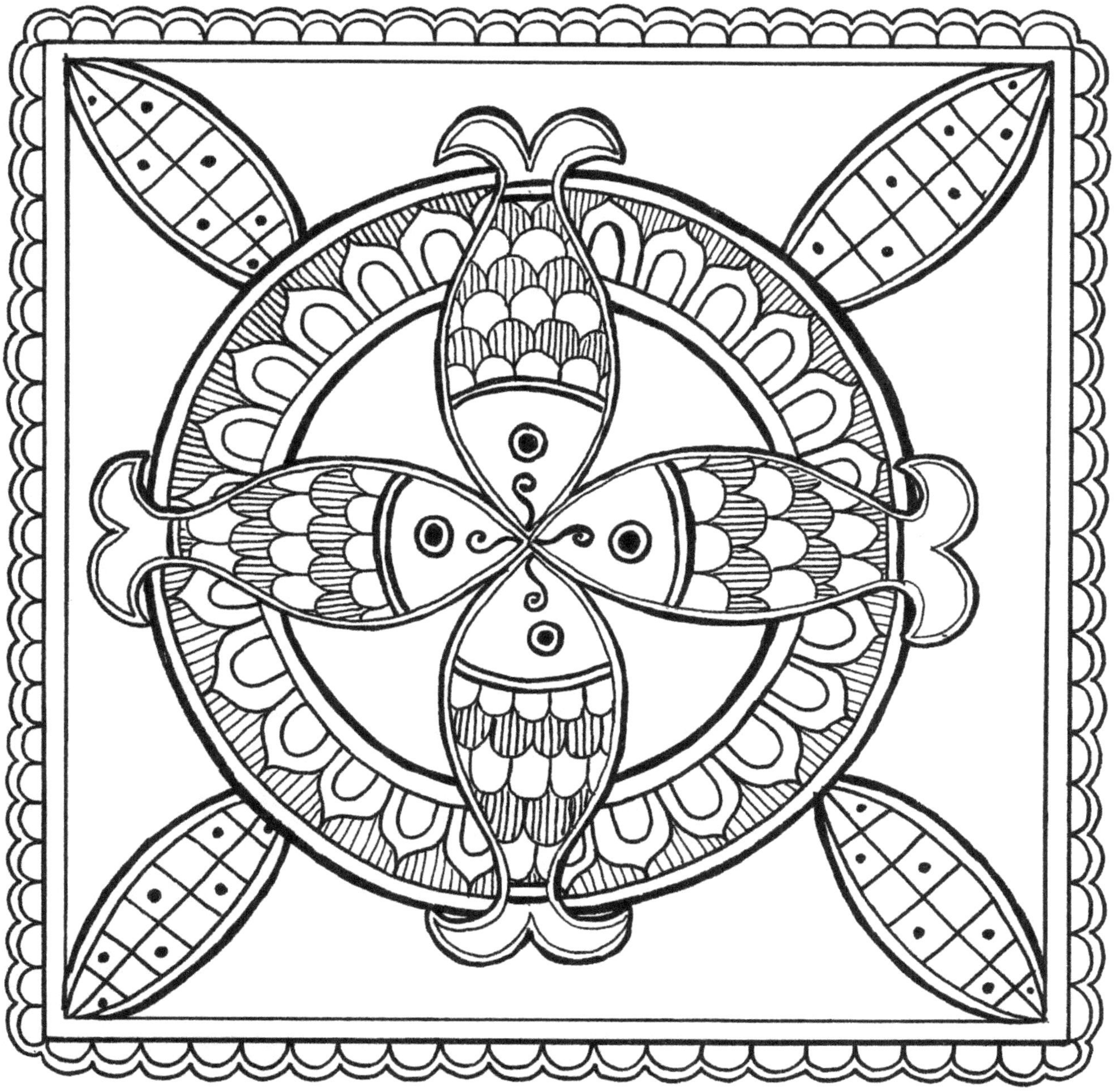

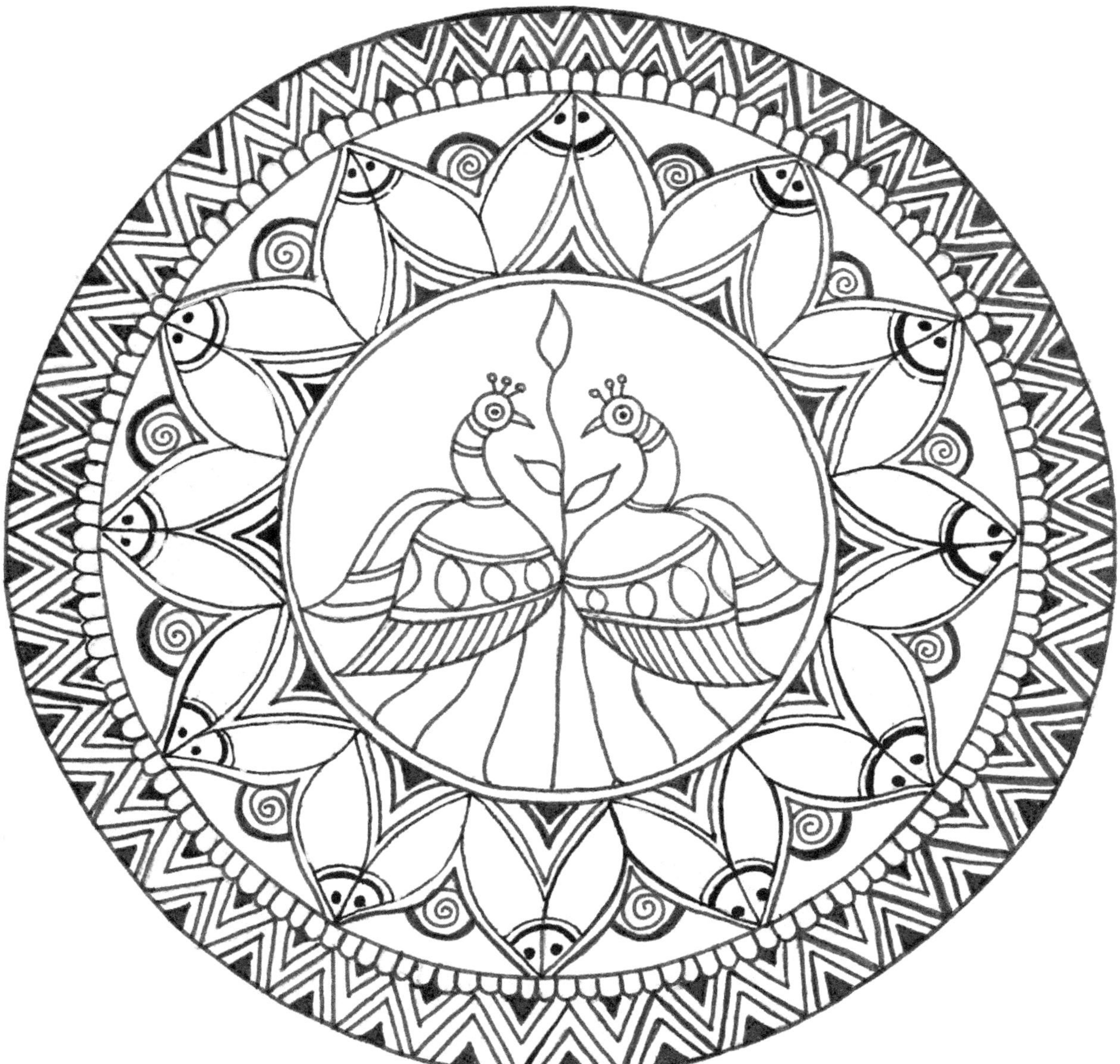

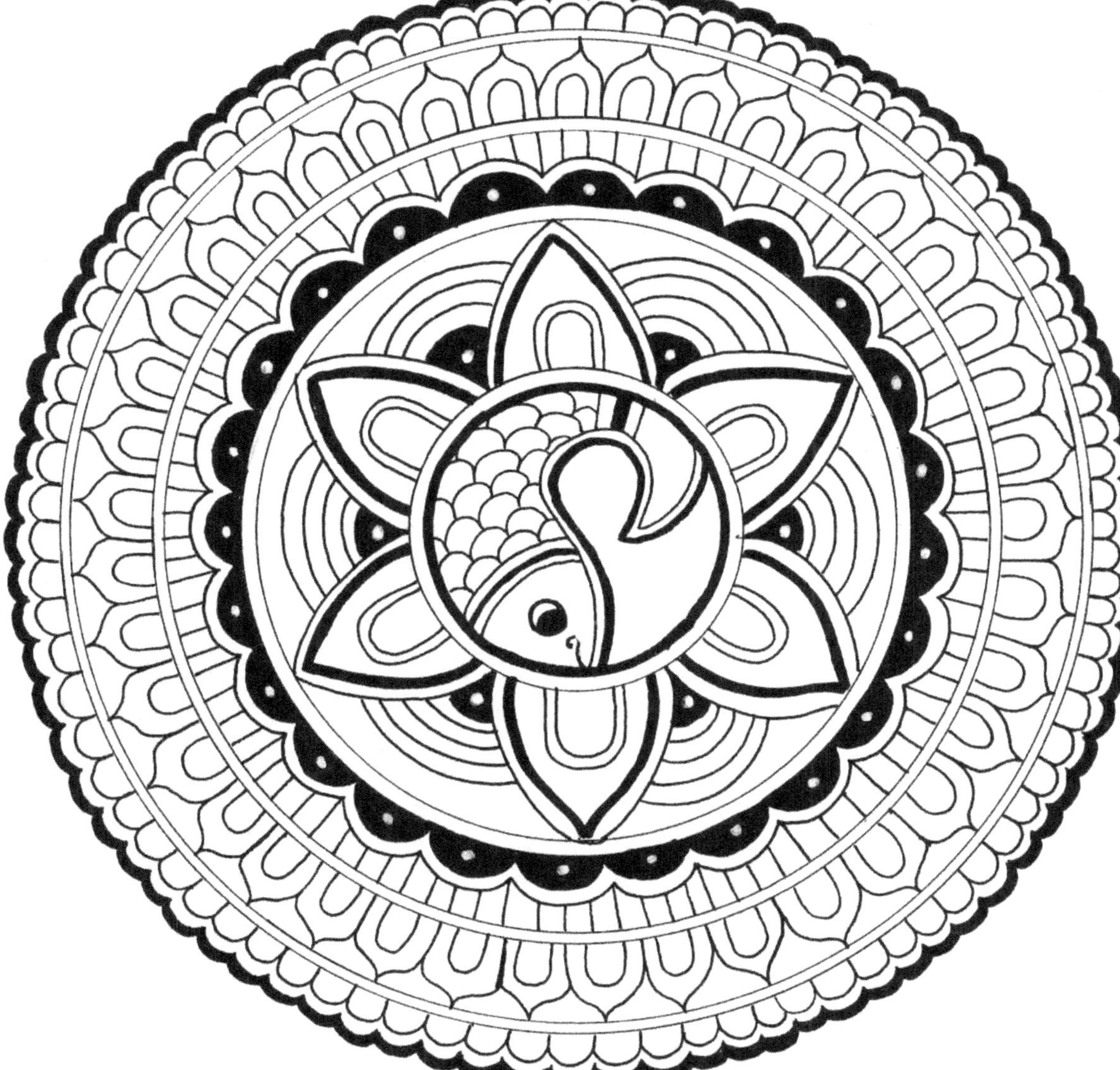

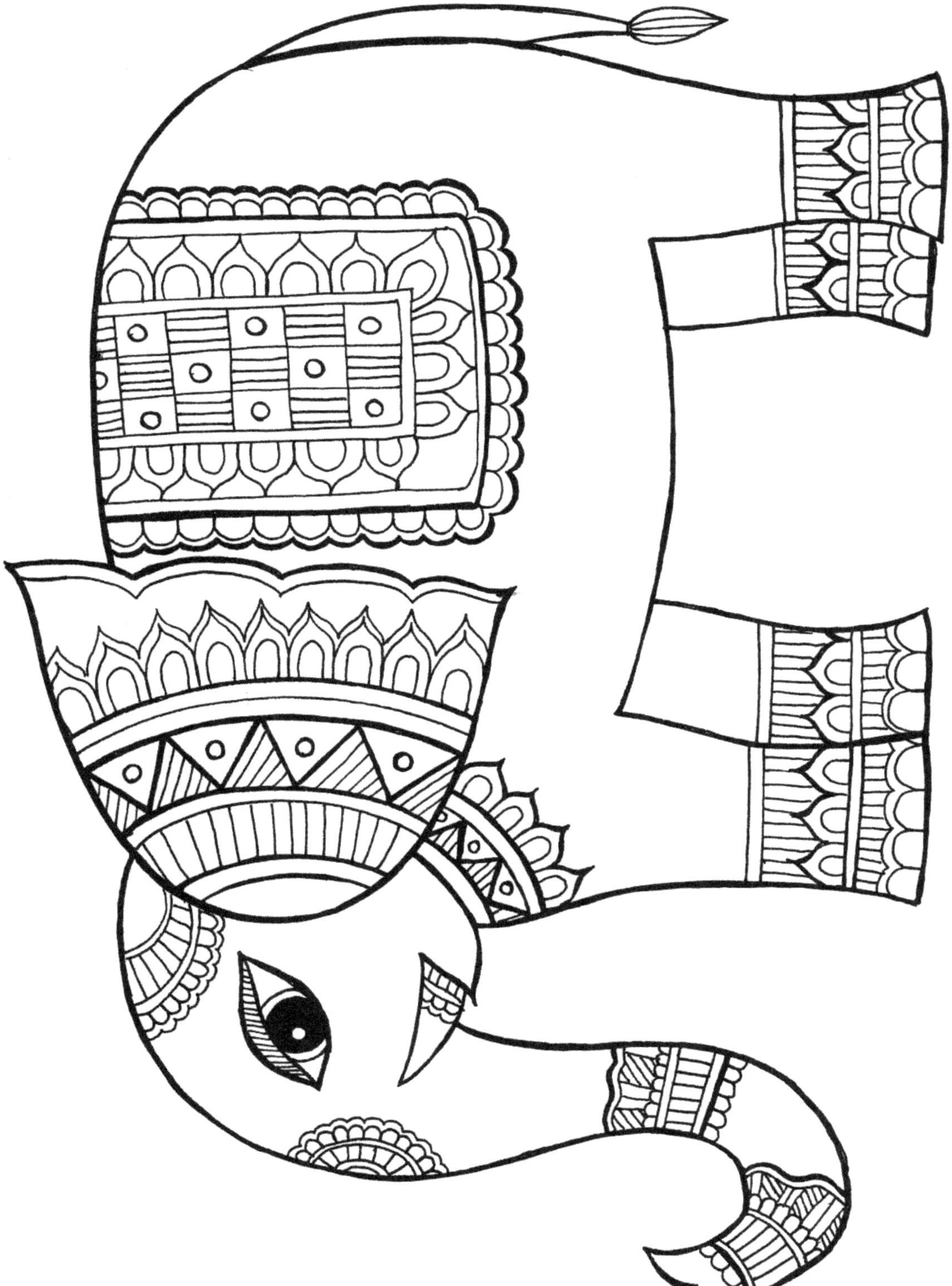

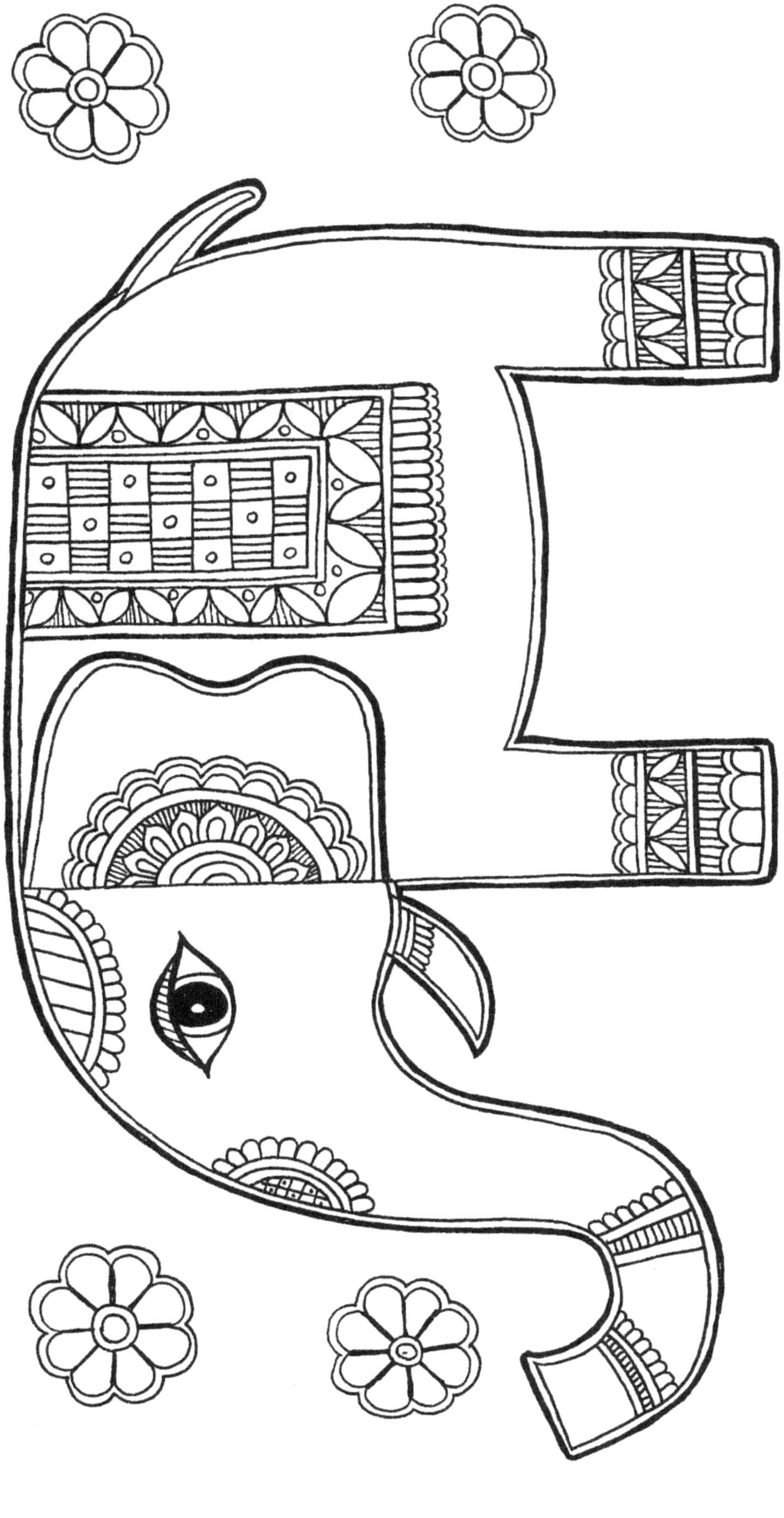

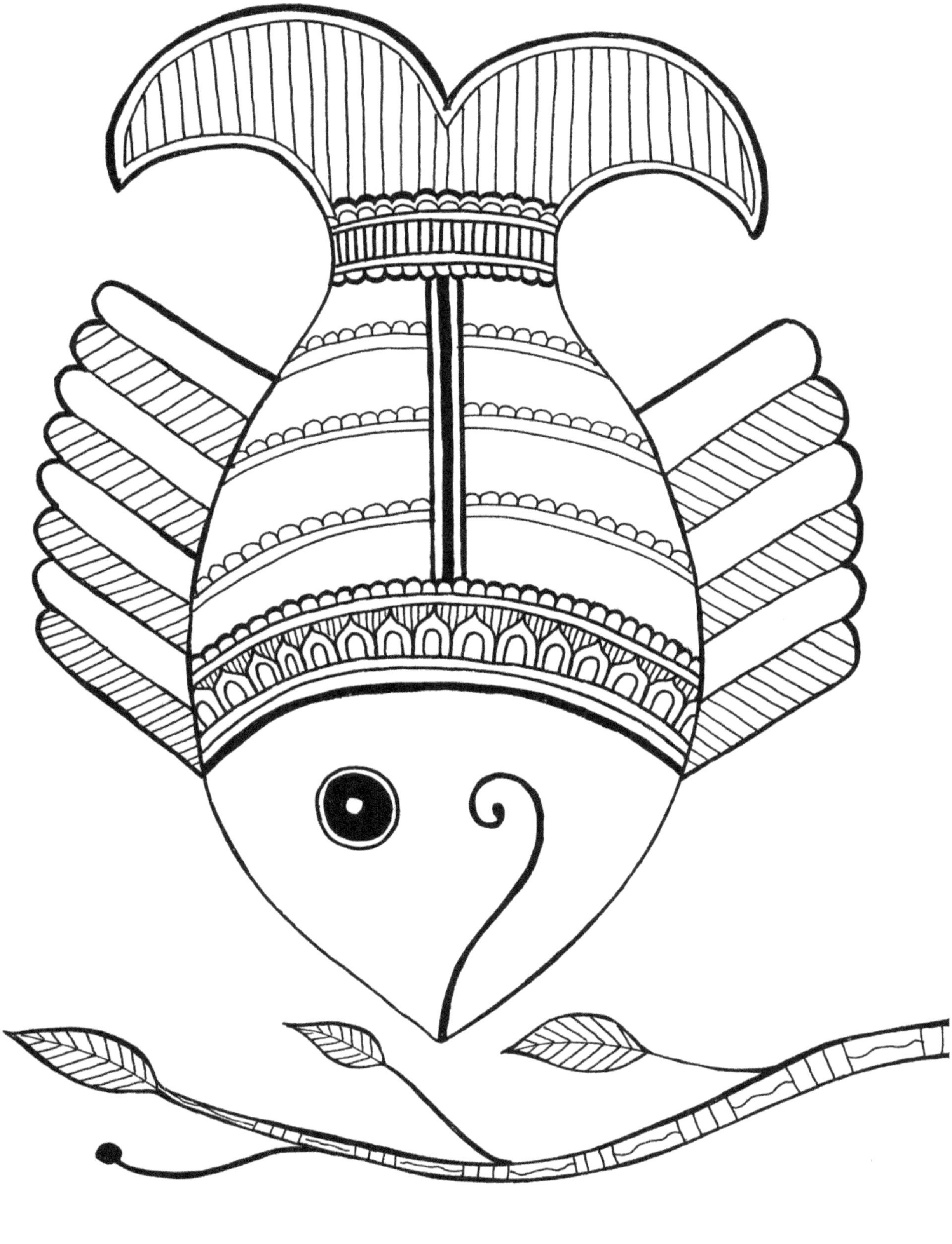

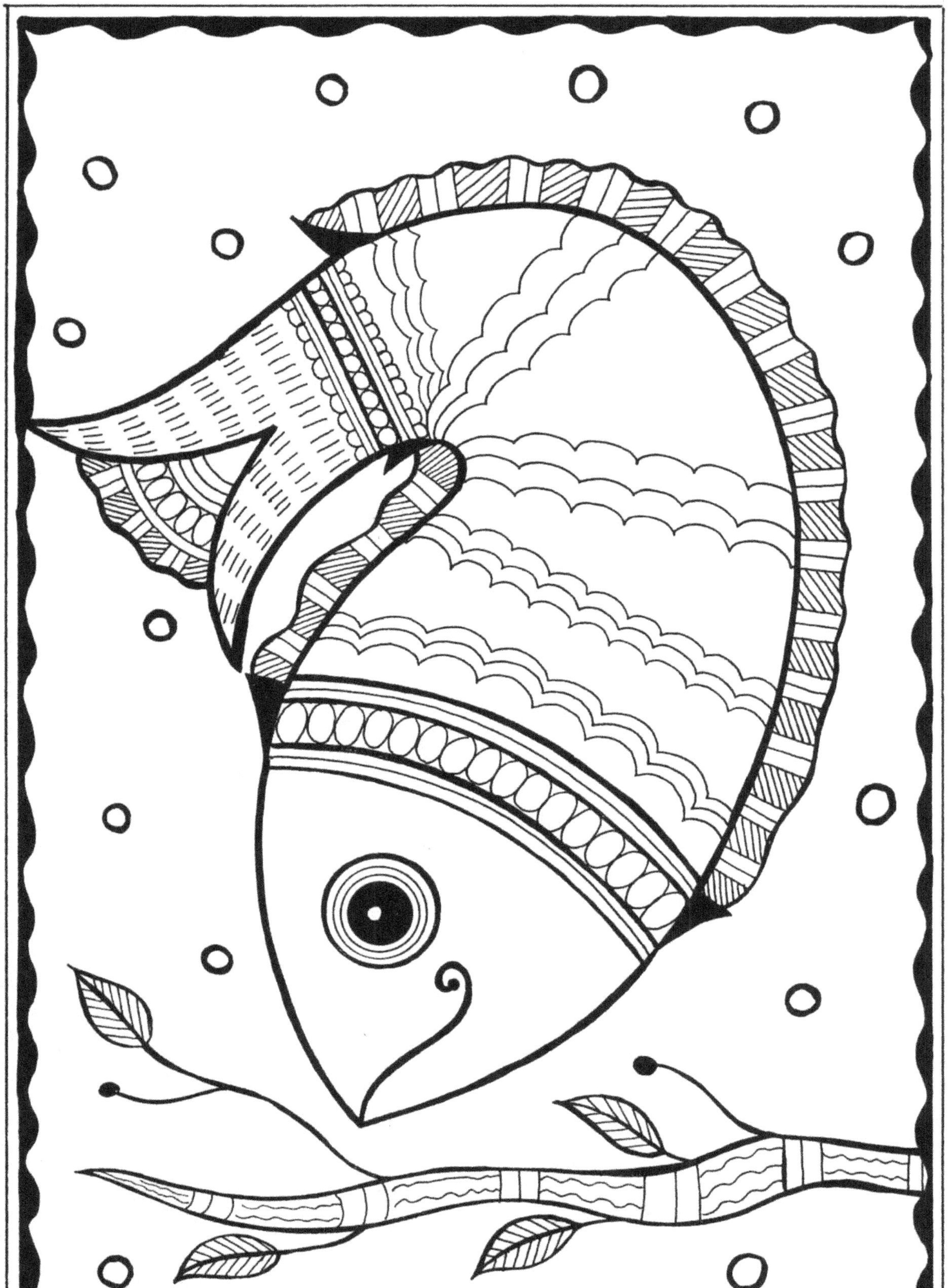

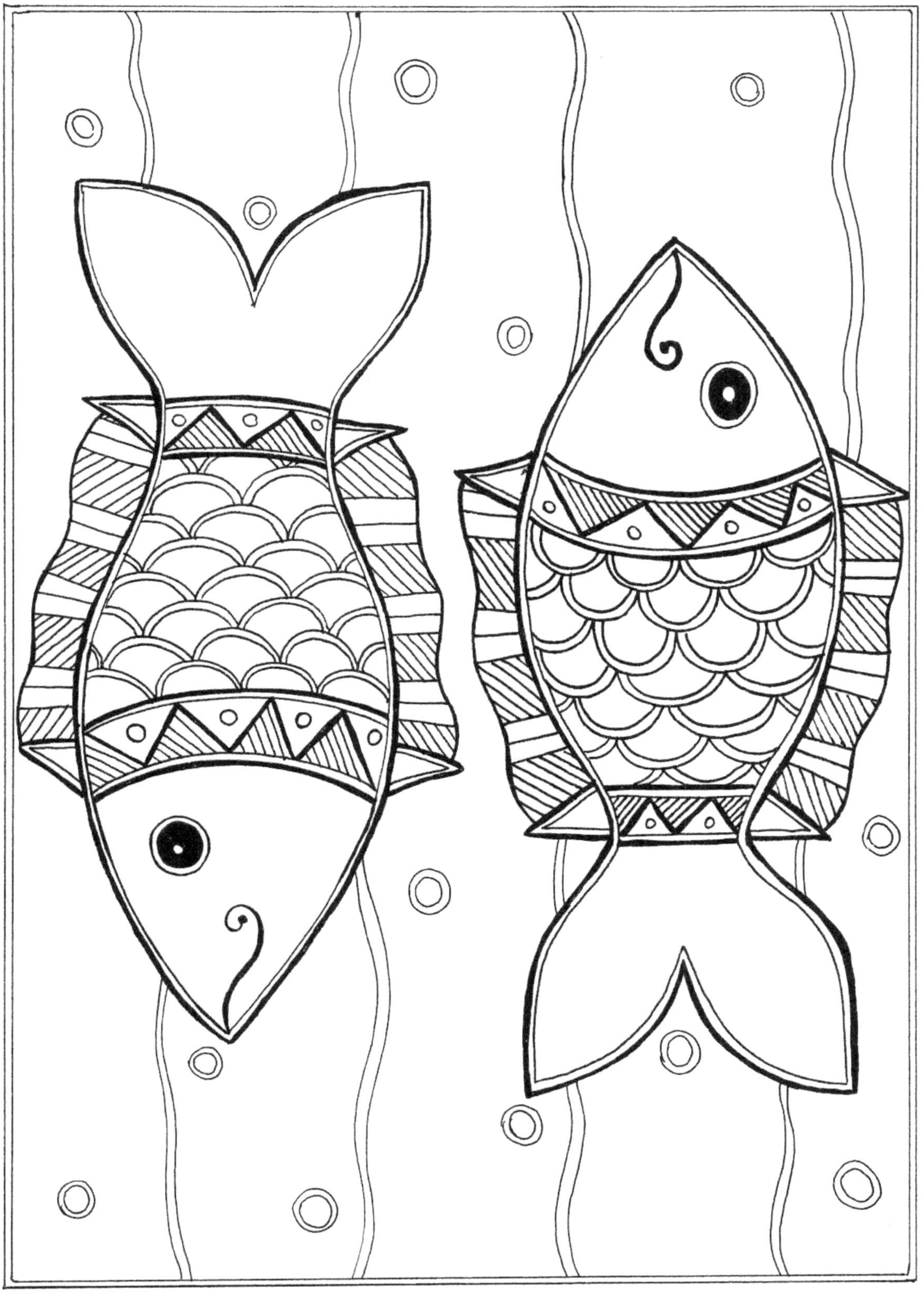

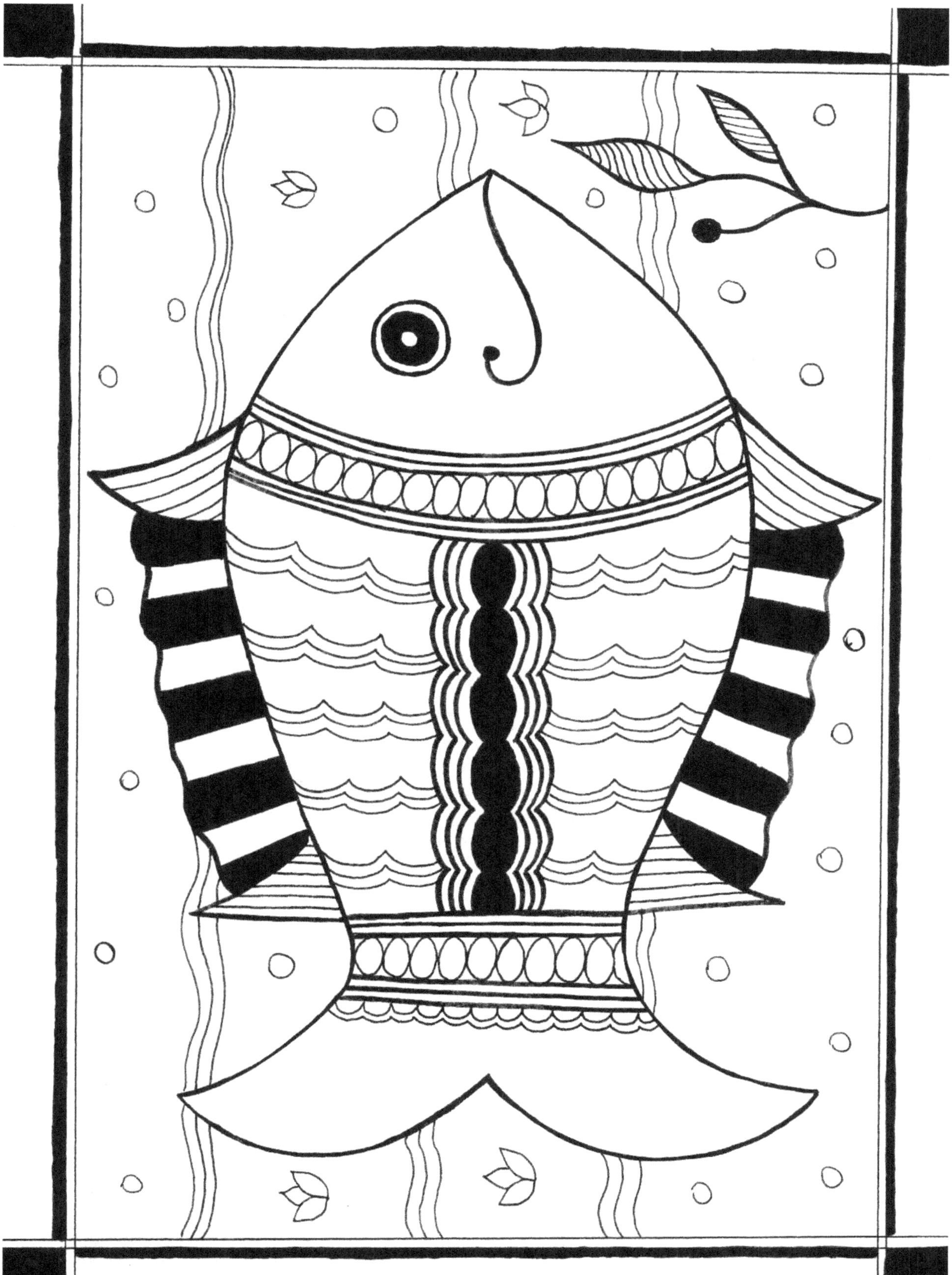

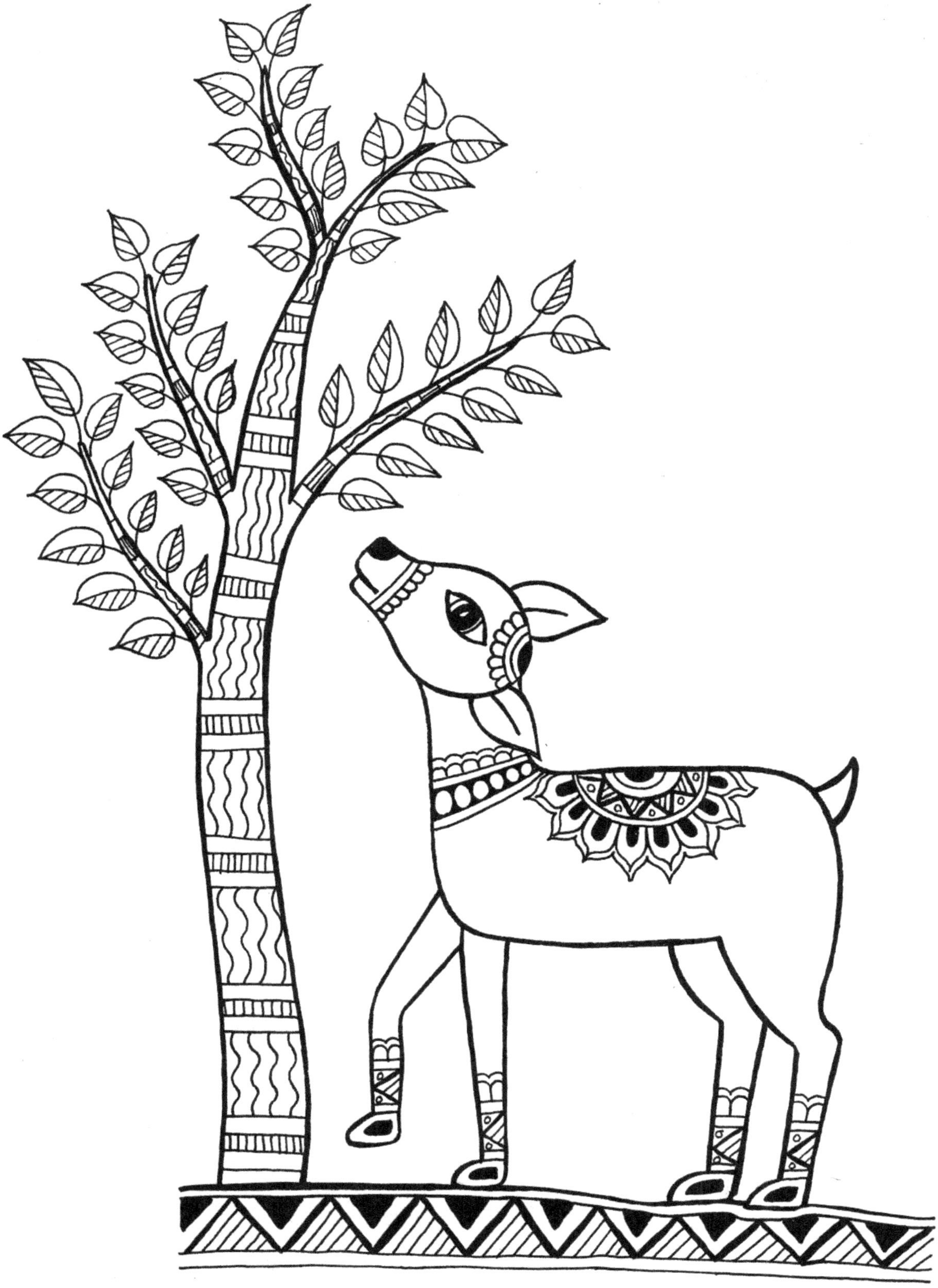

www.ingramcontent.com/pod-product-compliance
Lightning Source LLC
Chambersburg PA
CBHW081646220526
45468CB00009B/2571
* 9 7 8 1 9 8 4 9 5 6 4 9 1 *